Bamisaye Victor

BUT NOT ORPHANED

From Despair to Inspire

Vinnytsia
LLC "Nilan-LTD"
2016

bamisayevictor@yahoo.com

ISBN 978-966-924-292-1

CONTENTS

DEDICATION

I dedicate this book to God almighty

And

To the loving memory of my parents

Aare Ademola Bamisaye

And

Chief (mrs) Olukemi Bamisaye.

ACKNOWLEDGEMENTS

This story might not have been without the following people who contributed immensely to my life as a project.

To the woman I now call mother Mrs G.Y Omotade for her graciousness to take responsibility for me when no one else did.

To my father in the lord Rev. Dr Albert Kitcher, thanks for instilling in me and so many others the virtues to conquer the world and also giving me and the readers of this great work the privilege of accepting to foreword this manual, I have read it many times over and I am deeply inspired by them. God bless you some more.

To Bishop Noel Jones, albeit I haven't met you in person but I would err not to acknowledge how much I have learnt and I am still learning from you. Listening to you over the years did not stop at influencing me, it in fact revolutionised my thought process.

But Not Orphaned

 To my Friend who became brother, Ojo Anuoluwapo, notable among so many of his heroics is the fact not so many people knew I was once without a house because he made sure I wasn't homeless, with him I can say God puts people strategically in your life to be a consolation.

To Pastor Sunday Adelaja, I'm glad I met you and your teachings, they've helped instil in me the confidence that my dreams are not only valid but also borderless.

To my dear Chimzorom Uguru who has shouldered many extra burden that came with creating this book from typesetting, editing to also proof reading. Thank you.

To Pastor Joshua Ojuade for his great works in proof reading and building quotes out of this manuscript.

To Doctor Lade Adepoju for choosing to believe in me, thank you so much.

But Not Orphaned

To Doctors Emeordi Chidera, Oyedepo Faith and Asunbo Abayomi with you guys I have confirmed that strangers indeed do become family. Thanks for your tremendous support.

To Professor (Mrs) Geraldine Ugwuonah, Mr. Tony Ikharo and Mrs Opanuga for contributing their great quota to push me to achieve my dreams

And to everyone who contributed in one way or the other to the success of this book, I want to say a very big thank you.

But Not Orphaned

FOREWORD

"But Not Orphaned" in my view is not just a book, it is a Consciousness. It makes you take inventory of your life and purpose as you seek first God's Kingdom. The teachings, lessons, and encouragements in this book serves as a map to realization of identity and true self.

For those who do not know what tomorrow holds, this book will teach you and give you the tools to take hold of the future. You will understand your true purpose and know who you are.

Victor looks at death and loss from a fresh new perspective. This insight into how to turn pain into gain is a MUST LEARN AND PRACTICE for every youth and adult who missed it in their youth.

 Many people try to pull God in a box but not Victor. He teaches and encourages you to dismantle borders and restrictions and break free into your world of potential.

But Not Orphaned

This book is just the beginning of greater works to follow. I see manuals, booklets, plays, skits, movies emerging out of this book.

Thanks a lot Victor for sharing your gold with the world. You have made the word 'but' more meaningful and in its positive usage.

I'm glad to be a father, friend, mentor and much more to you. I look to the future with smiles because people of your calibre will keep the light shining. This is just the beginning.

Finally, I want to challenge every reader to read the whole book, practice the lessons and pass it on to someone you love and care about.

Dr. Albert S. L. Kitcher

World Transformation Church (Founder)

KAIROS Group Initiatives (CEO)

But Not Orphaned

PREFACE

But Not Orphaned was born out of the need to communicate with my generation and beyond, I have always considered myself to be the link between two generations which makes me a part of three different dispensations, I have received knowledge from the generation before me, I am living and experiencing the generation to which I was born and all of this I am and will pass down not just to this generation but to the ones to come.

As you read this book I'd like you to open your mind, ask God for understanding and that He through this material meet you at the point of need. The truth about But not orphaned is that it transcends its title and communicates even to people who are yet to lose a thing.

This book is the product of a conscious and intentional learning process that spanned over two years and even many more years of subconscious learning.

But Not Orphaned

It is my prayer that your testimonies will abound
after your encounter with the words written
therein and I'd be glad to share in that with you.

Bamisaye Victor

But Not Orphaned

Bamisaye Victor is a dynamic young man with a vision and a high sense of responsibility. A leader among his peers. I met him during my overseas posting in Ukraine and having worked closely with him in Crimea as one of the Nigerian students leaders and later in Lviv as the pioneer President of the Nigerian Students Association Ukraine (NSAU).

I can confidently say that Victor is a motivator and a selfless young man who loves to help and bring about solutions to problems anywhere he finds himself. With so much zeal and self-confidence, I was shocked to know that he had lost his father quite early and orphaned at a very critical time of his life when his mother also passed on a few years ago leaving him and his siblings to waddle through the deep waters of life. Yet, instead of being a victim, Victor chose to live out his name. He is indeed victorious. This book, "But not Orphaned", among other things, is a testimony to that fact. I know the seed of greatness dwells in him and as he continues to steadfastly nurture it, I am confident

But Not Orphaned

that Victor will bless his generation and make a great impact on many lives for the glory of God.

Mrs Ayo Luther-Ogbomode

Senior Counsellor (2013-2016)

Nigerian Embassy to Ukraine

But Not Orphaned

The search for a book on personal leadership is over! Dr Bamisaye Victor has captured it, simplified it and delivered it so we can live it and build it in others.

This book gives us an opportunity to look into the author's journey-spiritual, financial, academic and emotional. It inspires us with its life nuggets and comforts us with its resounding message: We are never orphans, even if the world forsakes us.

A must read

Dr. Oluwole Femi

Author "The Winning Edge"

But Not Orphaned

Before beginning this book, it would be of utmost value if you recognise that this book was not written to entertain or solicit sympathy. It is a life manual encoded with real life experiences and practical principles that would help you chart the course of your life to the fulfilling of your purpose despite upraising challenges and seemingly overwhelming oppositions.

 Bamisaye Victor is my Friend, Brother and Colleague thus if there's anyone that can give you a first-hand information about what He has gone through and much more the victories he has won through the application of the principles penned down in this book, I am qualified to do that having been together for the past five years. I congratulate you dear reader for getting this book in your hands, and as you read this book and digest its content, Victory is inevitable.

 Ojo Anuoluwapo.

Pastor ZOE-IN-YOU CHURCH,

Lviv, Ukraine.

CHAPTER 1

Have you ever been in a situation where tomorrow looked so bleak and the only thing you knew was that tomorrow would come but of every other thing, especially yourself, you were unsure?

Have you ever looked at yourself and your surrounding and made up your mind it was game up?

The truth about life is that the ordinary man can only see today and cannot live beyond the present. That does not rule out the fact that he has dreams and aspirations or that he has beliefs. The ordinary man becomes shell-shocked many times when his aspirations and dreams are betrayed by the happenings in his life that are obviously beyond his control. Then he feels out of control and proceeds to resign to fate, which proves to be the first step of his undoing as this puts him in an angle where the question becomes, who is responsible for his outcomes?

But Not Orphaned

His situation? The people around him? Himself?

The situations around a man are things he may not be able to influence from source. Nevertheless, I believe that prayer has the ability to change things although there are times when God Himself allows some circumstances into our lives that we cannot question just as scripture says in the book of **Isaiah 29:16**

"Surely your turning of things upside down shall be esteemed as the potter's clay: for shall the work say of him that made it, He made me not? or shall the thing framed say of him that framed it, He had no understanding."

And reiterated in **Romans 9:21** thus:

Hath not the potter power over the clay, of the same lump to make one vessel unto honour, and another unto dishonour?

But in this case, our consolation is in the scripture that says: all things work together for good to them that love God and are called according to His purpose. **Romans 8:28**.

And we know that all things work together for good to them that love God, to them who are the called according to his purpose.

Let me show you just a little more, if you will stay on **Romans 8** beginning this time from **verse 19.**

For the earnest expectation of the creature waiteth for the manifestation of the sons of God.

Let's observe the progression. **Verse 20** particularly says

For the creature was made subject to vanity, not willingly, but by reason of him who hath subjected the same in hope.

So here, we see that the situation around the creation wasn't because the creation was responsible but because it was "subjected"– subjection denotes force, to be under obedience of a thing, to be subdued – and it seems as though the whole idea was working against the creation. I

But Not Orphaned

want you to imagine how comfortable subjection can be. Ironic right? To rub salt into the injury, the subjection was unto vanity; vanity means nothing, futility, emptiness.

Imagine I come to your house and forcefully eject you, leaving you with no alternative. How wicked could I be? What would be going through your mind against me?

But the intrigue, the suspense, the contradiction, however it may seem, still lies in this verse when it says this "subjection" is by reason of the same person who did it in "hope". Hope? What hope? How can I see vanity and you're telling me about hope? These two are antithetical to one another; in fact they are irreconcilable parallel opposites.

Back to the narrative I started earlier, imagine that after you have been evicted and homeless for 4 weeks, someone else comes to tell you that someone (that being me) actually had it in mind to move you into a duplex without telling you it is me. Again, what will be your reaction? The last intrigue here is that "I" am hidden within the context of the whole situation such that you really may not know it is me. So who am I? The verse said, "But by reason of him who had subjected the same in hope". To put this in an equation, it may look something like this:

A(±)B=C

C+A*D=E

When D is a subset of X, find X.

A is you.

(±) B is whatever is added or removed from your life.

=C is the situation created.

D represents Hope.

=E is your recreated reality

X is the origin of the hope.

But Not Orphaned

Now, there are two forces that seem greater than man and that on a rapid initial diagnosis we suspect to have the ability to subject creation.

They are:

1. God
2. The adversary (the devil)

The latter seemed to be the best option knowing that creature was made subject to vanity but he fell short of the description after the verse went on to mention hope. Just as John 10:10a says.

The thief cometh not, but for to steal, and to kill, and to destroy

There is no hope in stealing, neither in killing nor in destruction. All of these bring pain and despair. If you have doubts, then ask someone who has lost something or someone about the feeling that came with it; ask someone who had his possession demolished about the state of his mind after the process, especially if there was no compensation made.

So it could only have been God. It is only God who puts hope at the end of every situation He allows and this hope is received by all those who are submitted to Him. So when you check verse 21 of Romans 8, you'll see the hope for which He had subjected the creation to vanity.

 Because the creature itself also shall be delivered from the bondage of corruption into the glorious liberty of the children of God.

A lot of times, just because where we are is not comfortable, we conclude that it is not the right place and we ought not to be there.
Just take a minute and consider Jesus, the only begotten son of the father. One looking on the periphery, would wonder why His father would send Him to a disorganized earth at the expense of a glittering heaven in the first place; and on getting deeper, would question yet again, why He would have subjected Him to the vanity of death,

especially one at the cross following a series of bodily tortures and abuse. But a master planner, who sees the end from the beginning, had the plan of redemption hidden in the suffering and consequent death of His son.

He was there in the tomb the first day and no hope was seen, He was there on the second day and we didn't know what He was doing; but on the third day as 1 Corinthians 15 puts it, He gained victory over sin, the graveyard and death so one can only conclude that His death wasn't a subjection to vanity after all.

55 O death, where is thy sting? O grave, where is thy victory?

56 The sting of death is sin; and the strength of sin is the law.

57 But thanks be to God, which giveth us the victory through our Lord Jesus Christ.

Consider Joseph to whom God had made the promise through his dream, of a hope for his future and note how incidents began to unfold that were antagonistic to this hope. His coat of many colours was ripped off, there was a deliberation to kill him by those he held dearest, he suffered betrayal from those who were closest to him and for whom he had such regard he shared his dreams with them. Joseph couldn't have told just anybody, he could only tell his family but they were the very ones who would put him in a well and sell him to slave traders, who would in turn trade him in the slave market. Slavery would become his reality and within that reality, he'd have another super reality; he would be seduced and consequently implicated for being righteous enough to insist on loving God beyond the pleasures he could get, he would be sent to prison for an offence he didn't commit and in fact, things seemingly would begin moving from bad to worse. Something must have told him on the inside that the worst was yet to come. As I write, I try to put myself in Joseph's place, to feel the vibes of the circumstances surrounding him, to tap into his emotional state and I just feel like shouting in his stead, "Where is my dream? Where is my hope?

But Not Orphaned

Where is my God?" I wonder if he did scream out so because you and I probably would.

Your inability to see the full picture does not mean God is not working on your behalf. Joseph knew little that the well was not a wrong place but rather the perfect place for him to be at that moment; he might not have understood but God had a reason for allowing him to be sold as a slave.

Bishop Noel Jones said in one of his teachings that the essence of Joseph going to prison was because Potiphar has no inroad to Pharaoh's palace. Therefore, to get him to Pharaoh's house, God had to bring him near someone who had contacts with Pharaoh and that happened to be Pharaoh's butler, who was imprisoned at that same time.

God knows how to use transient negativities to bring you into permanent positivity.

One of the problems we have in believing God in the midst of our situations is that we already have a set parameter of how we think God should operate both in our lives and around us; and most

But Not Orphaned

times God being God operates outside of our standards. Then we conclude that this cannot be God and because we did not recognize the time of our visitation because of our limited rationale of how we understand and think God should operate, some of us come to the conclusion that God must have forgotten us, others that He doesn't even exist. But it is quite simple.

Let me put it in three sentences.

1. You cannot rationalize how God operates; it takes a revelation.
2. God is not boxed-in by or into your conceptualization of him, He is just God.
3. God is beyond our reason[ing] but yet appeals to our reason[ing].

This applies to our daily lives. When we have some expectations, issues and prayers that we lay at God's feet and when we do not get the results we want, we tend to give up our faith in God but until you realize that He who made you loves you and will always want what's best for you and that you are limited in knowledge of realities especially as you do not know what may happen in the next second but God does, then you would come to the conclusion that He is working everything out for your good not only for now but also for your tomorrow. This is an essential thing that the psalmist understood and declared in Psalm 23:4.

Yea, though I walk through the valley of the shadow of death, I will fear no evil: for thou art with me; thy rod and thy staff they comfort me.

Have you ever considered the strong words used in that verse?

1. Valley: A valley is a type of land formation. A valley is a long "depression" (or low part) in the land, between two higher parts which might be hills or mountains. Valleys often start as a downward fold between two upward folds in the surface of the Earth. Many of us like the psalmist believe that the high places belong to us; it is not a wrong

mentality but is meant to be your reality as purported in Deuteronomy 32:13

He made him ride on the high places of the earth, that he might eat the increase of the fields; and he made him to suck honey out of the rock, and oil out of the flinty rock.

And reiterated by the psalmist in Psalms 18:33

He maketh my feet like hinds' feet, and setteth me upon my high places.

Once more, the prophet Isaiah prophesied it in Isaiah 58:14

Then shalt thou delight thyself in the LORD; and I will cause thee to ride upon the high places of the earth, and feed thee with the heritage of Jacob thy father: for the mouth of the LORD hath spoken it.

So the psalmist was saying in psalm 23 when he used the word "valley" that even though he was at the lowest part of the earth, which was contradictory to his belief that he owned the high places, he would fear no evil.

2. Shadow: A dark shape that appears on a surface when someone or something moves between the surface and a source of light; an area of darkness created when a source of light is blocked. In other words shadow can be described as the reality in the absence of light. And light in this case is the epitome of hope, which is why people always encourage themselves to look forward to seeing the light at the end of the tunnel. The psalmist was saying however, "I don't need to look forward to a light at the end of the tunnel when I have the light with me in the tunnel. Even if He doesn't shine, just knowing that He is there will keep me going."

3. Death: It simply means the absence of life. The psalmist's thought was in this line, even if all that I am doing seemingly starts loosing life and the tree upon which my hope is anchored dries up, I wouldn't even be

But Not Orphaned

startled as long as I know He (the life Himself who also is the life giver) is there with me.

So you can now put the three together and see that the psalmist was saying this: even though I am in the lowest of place where there is no light and everything is dead, I will fear no evil for thou (who make all things beautiful in its time) art with me.

The psalmist wouldn't complain about his situation. His only concern was one thing with which he wouldn't mind anything; all he cared to know was the presence of God in all of his situations. You have to get to that point where you can say, "Lord, even if you take me to hell there's no problem. Just don't leave me." As long as the presence of God is assured, it doesn't matter your location, you have nothing to fret about.

Moses wasn't concerned about how many wars he had to fight or how many oceans he had to cross. All he would say was that if the Lord didn't go with them, they wouldn't proceed.

Exodus 33:15.

But Not Orphaned

And he said unto him, If thy presence go not with me, carry us not up hence.

Before and even upon the cross, Jesus wasn't concerned about the fate of His container (body). He only shouted when He bore the sins of the world and God wouldn't look at Him (because the eyes of the Lord shall not behold iniquity). At that point, He was in despair not because He had been speared, scourged or crowned with thorns but because He didn't feel the presence of God in that little while.

The presence of God must become your rallying point in every situation.

Three Hebrew men held unto their faith which led them to an unpleasant fate, a circumstance they couldn't control, a situation no man could stop. If the outcome had been different, an interesting question would have been asked. Why did God not show up? Why did He not stop the king? What a master planner! He sure knows what to do and when to do it.

But Not Orphaned

The glory is always in the completion of the process.

One interesting thing and worthy of note about the story is that while they were thrown into the burning furnace and were dancing in it, those who threw them in did not survive the heat.

Have you ever been in a situation so deep that those who didn't even go through a quarter of what you went through did not survive? Have you ever been in a situation where those who put you there couldn't even live to complete the process they started, they put you in between the hooks and you still had the victory?

Oh boy, I know how that feels. It happens when God is present. Did you take note that in that fire, there was a fourth man? Who can put you in a fire when you've got the Holy Ghost fire on your inside? These men were dancing. They had a different reality even though their situation did not change.

But Not Orphaned

When the presence of God steps into your situation, He does not necessarily change your situation but He definitely will change your reality.

Did you notice also that there was a storm and a people on the ship who did not recognize that the presence of God (Christ) was on board? What did they do? They were scared, they were very afraid they couldn't handle the situation. They were overwhelmed by the reality they had. But in that ship was a man, who knew who He was. He didn't behave like them. As a matter of fact, the bible recorded that He was sleeping. He was at rest and when they woke Him up, He simply said, "Peace, be still." The presence of God changes the definition of your situation.

YOUR STORM BECOMES PEACE, YOUR TEARS OF SORROW BECOME TEARS OF JOY, EVEN YOUR CREATIVITY BECOMES A TRAINING GROUND AND YOUR SHAME BECOMES GOD'S GLORY.

Therefore, the presence of God is the game-changer that not only works on your spirit, but more importantly on your mind. The scripture says therefore where the presence of God is, there is liberty. Often, we confuse liberty for freedom. You can be set free but not liberated. Freedom is an expression; liberty is an impression i.e. it is an inward acknowledgement. Freedom is about bodily movement, liberty deals with the mind. Maybe you are in the prison, the presence of God may not guarantee your release (freedom) but it definitely will activate your liberty. Liberty then leads to peace.

Peace has been defined as absence of war, trouble, fracas, or the presence of serenity, calm and order. While I do not dispute these characteristics of peace I'd have to say it is incomplete.

Because peace does not deal with the outside, peace reconciles the inner part of man. Peace is a manifestation of a greater presence suppressing or overshadowing the reality of a man in his situation.

Peace is the state of calmness, serenity and composure even in the presence of war, trouble or problems. It is interesting to know that peace is not an event, it is not a destination; it is a process, it is a journey. I can only measure how much a thing can resist by introducing an irritant. Therefore, the measure of a man's peace is how much trouble he gets in. You can claim to have peace as much as you want to, but I'll like to see your reaction to seemingly bad news. I want to see how you move on when everything around you seems to be regressing. I want to see how joyous you remain in the face of economic crises.

It is also important to note that your peace is dependent on your insurance. Many people have their insurance in their money and so when money dwindles, they lose their peace. Others have it in their spouse and when the human in them (the spouse) shows up, they lose their peace. Many have theirs in their work and when work wears them out, they lose their peace. What is your insurance? I have mine in the word of God. So, a lot may change but the word of God remains hence I do not lose my peace.

But Not Orphaned

On April 20th 2014 at about 4 o'clock AM, my phone rang and on the other end of the line was my younger brother, who informed me that we had just lost our mother. Having lost our father seven years earlier, this meant we had become parentless. Like every other human would be upon hearing such news, I was down. However, it was a Sunday so I got ready as usual and headed to church where I danced like I always did. I had joy on my inside although my situation did not change; my reality was different. On Monday, I went to class, related with everyone and carried on with my activities, all as I would usually do.

 Judging by my carriage, anyone who knew what had happened might have assumed that I did not love my parents. But oh, how I loved those two! Yet, I did not mourn like those who do not have hope. My everyday schedule continued without alteration for three weeks. On the third week, an old school mate who also happened to study in my university was called by his mother inquiring about my welfare, my disposition and my behaviour to decipher whether or not I had been informed of my mother's death. My friend assured his mother that I way okay and nothing was wrong and that was when his mother shared with him the news of what had happened, telling him to be cautious and wise in breaking the news to me. When he finally called me, he said he just wanted to say hi and check up on me and how I was faring. Knowing already what his intentions were, I simply replied that I was fine and in the casual Yoruba tone added, "Femi, this one you're calling me today, I hope all is well." Unable to bring himself to complete his mission, Femi responded, "No, it's nothing" to which I replied, "Okay, take care!"

Femi informed the head pastor of my church as at then. However, prior to this time, I had already invited one of the assisting pastors for a walk in the park during which I shared with him the situation, eliciting surprise from him at how my demeanour had gone unaltered and I had acted normal for three weeks like all was well. So, when the head pastor summoned her colleagues for a plan on the best way to break the news to me, they were shocked at the revelation of the pastor whom I already told as he said to them "Victor knows already! He has known for three weeks now." When on the fourth Sunday I testified in church, disbelief overwhelmed everyone.

Now, it should be noted that I wasn't trying to be strong. Although many did say, "Victor you are a strong man," the truth is I wasn't trying to be. If I had tried to be strong, I would have been smiling outside but dying inside but I was getting stronger by the day on my inside and the secret was and is the presence of God. Scripture says, *IN THE PRESENCE OF GOD, THERE IS FULLNESS OF JOY*. This was how it worked for me. **John 1:1**

In the beginning was the Word, and the Word was with God, and the Word was God.

I was full of the word – very full – before the situation, so I didn't actually wait on or for anyone before I got my comfort because I had the presence of the word (God) in me; the word fulfilled the promise in me. The bible says, "The words that I speak unto you, they are SPIRIT and they are LIFE." So where and when no one could help me emotionally, I had—by use of the word— trained my mind. I had understood the essence of submitting to God so that right there, as weak as I was, His strength was made perfect in my weakness. So I realized, and this you have to remind yourself, that my weakness – being my situation – did not have to change at the instance of the perfection of his strength in me but tarrying for a little while, waiting on God for just a little longer, believing the report that says, "faithful is he who began a good work in me to complete it until the day of Christ", believing that if God be for me nothing can be (prevail) against me, holding unto the word that says, "many are the afflictions of the righteous but the Lord delivers him from them all"; all of these would change my reality and in time, my reality would change my situation for scripture says: HE MAKES ALL THINGS BEAUTIFUL IN ITS TIME. As aforementioned, I have to reiterate once again that the presence of God does not

But Not Orphaned

necessarily change your situation, but it will change your reality.

The reason many of us do not survive the situations we could have easily walked over is not because they are too big to conquer, it is simply because we have a distorted reality. Have you considered Zerubabel and the mountain? The bible says, "Who art thou oh mountain, before Zerubabel, the king? Thou shalt be made plain." Here's the situation: there is a mountain, a mountain of difficulties, of failure, of hate, of regression, of ill health, of financial instability; you can name the mountains in your life. I have had some, do have some, and will still have some. Challenges are a part of life and are bound to rise. Problems will never cease but in all, they are merely situations.

The reality of Zerubabel was that no matter what name the mountain bore, no matter its height or slope – whatever its characteristics or descriptions were – it would be made plain. So, each time Zerubabel saw a mountain, he did not fret, he was not frightened but just kept moving, full of life, hopeful. Zerubabel did not look back just because he saw a mountain. Listen to me dear, you are more than Zerubabel; you've got inside of you what Zerubabel had outside of him. Yeah, the situation is that problems exist but the reality is that SOLUTIONS ABOUND. You are as great as the quality of the opposition you overcome. Show me the last enemy you defeated and I will know how great you have become. The only reason you face what you may be facing right now is because you can overcome it. The only determining factor would be "your reality".

I must tell you this; there are two levels of truth.

1. The judgment of senses.
2. Your revelation.

Your senses judge and confirm your situations. For example when you feel sick, feel a headache, see your bank account red, hear some bad news and so on, they are true; your senses hardly lie. What you feel may not be incorrect but I can authoritatively tell you that it is most times incomplete because your revelation is truer. Your revelation is the interpretation of the word of God by the spirit of God to address your situation per time. Hence, even when your body feels sick and your revelation says by His stripes you've been made whole and goes further to say that "strangers shall harken to thy voice" and flee away from their hiding places, then all you just have to do is let go of the lesser truth and cling unto the higher one.

From 2005 when I was writing my Junior Secondary School Examination until 2010 when I wrote my first semester examination as a first year medical student in Bingham University Nigeria, there was never an examination period during which I did not fall sick. As a matter of fact, I wrote my Senior Secondary School Examination in pains but the climax was being infected with chicken pox in the first semester exam of my first year. This hindered me from performing as well as I should have academically. But when I resumed for my second semester, my reality changed because I had a revelation and so I said a little prayer that has changed my life ever since. I reasoned that if Jesus was a man on earth and he was never recorded to be sick, he must have had a particular type of blood flowing through his veins and so I asked that the same blood flow through me. All I noticed for the rest of that semester was that I did not fall sick and I wrote my exams successfully but not until I took a blood test while processing my visa to Ukraine did I notice that my genotype had actually changed from AS to AA and ever since, I became alien to medical prescriptions (drugs). Thus, I was set free by a higher truth and delivered by engaging this truth (revelation). The truth must be told that I still do feel headaches sometimes and that can be attributed to stress. So in wisdom and understanding of my reality, I just calmly sleep and wake up strong. I do not abuse my reality of health by subjecting myself to undue stress. I eat when necessary and take adequate rest after a stressful time. Many times, even in your reality created by the word of God, you need wisdom, "common sense".

The presence of God is a non-negotiable essential for without it, we'll amount to nothing. Jesus, while preparing His disciples for His departure, said in **John 14:18**

I will not leave you comfortless: I will come to you.

The word "comfortless" there comes from the word "orphanos" which means orphaned, and He continued the statement by saying, I will come to you. **Verses 19 and 20** give a clearer view of the eschatological part of **verse 18**.

Yet a little while, and the world seeth me no more; but ye see me: because I live, ye shall live also.
At that day ye shall know that I am in my Father, and ye in me, and I in you.

I want you to understand today that it is a mistake for you to be looking for God inside your situation.

But Not Orphaned

God is on your inside. When you are in a situation, just look on your inside; in there dwells God. Scripture says God is able to do exceedingly, abundantly above what you can think or imagine according to the power that works "IN" you. Scripture says if the spirit that raised Jesus from death lives "IN" you, he will quicken even your mortal body. My question is, when you look on your inside, who do you see? Let me tell you, in **1John 4:4** when John was admonishing the saints, he made a great statement.

Ye are of God, little children, and have overcome them: because greater is he that is in you, than he that is in the world

Note that in **John 14:19**, Jesus had said that when the world wouldn't see him, you would because he lives in you. I want you to notice that John couldn't have made such a statement when Jesus was alive because when Jesus was alive, the greatest was in the world and the statement would have been incorrect, null and void but when Jesus changed position and moved from the world to the inside of them who believed in Him, He no longer was in the world. Hence, John knew that he was carrying inside of him the greatest virtue, greatest power, greatest name there is and so when he looked outwardly, there was nothing to make him fret. There was nothing to keep him afraid. He knew, just like Paul, that if God be for us there is no one to be against us. He knew, like the prophet Elisha (speaking to his servant, who before then, could only see on the outside the number of soldiers that had come up against them) not to be afraid for those who are with us are more than our rivals.

There is a witnessing that should be going on in your spirit right now. The equation is quite simple. The manifest glory of God dwells in you. You are a God-carrier, situations cannot deter you, and circumstances cannot stop you. What I want you to know is that it doesn't matter what is on your outside, all that matters is who you are and have on your inside. I want you to know that whatever your outcome is, you should never blame your situation. As long as you are in line with God, everything is according to plan. It will all turn out well. You don't need to understand what is happening; all you need to know is who is making things happen for you. As for you, who have not been in line with God, it's never too late. God is the one who can make your yester-mess a morrow-message and turn your disgrace history into "this grace" story. It is only God who can redeem your past and present wrongs, and secure you a goodly heritage for your future. I want you to know that it may take time to straighten out a knot, it may take pain to excise a tumour, but God will take you from there. From where you had it over, he'll make your situation a consolation and your test a testimony.

I pray for you as you read that every situation keeping you at bay is sorted out right now.

CHAPTER 2

YOU MAY OR MAY NOT HAVE PEOPLE AROUND BUT YOU'RE NOT ORPHANED.

One truth we have to deal with is the fact that we'll always have to relate with people and the people with whom we relate tend to set the path and direction that our lives may take. It is often said, "show me your friend and I'll tell you who you are." It is only natural that you'd be defined by your association.

No doubt, people contribute to who we are and are going to be. According to an old adage, "It takes a couple to birth a child, but the whole village to train that child." Society (made up of people) has its own influence on our growth and the values we hold on to. It, in no little way, has effects on the standard of morals we have. Hence, we have become in one way or the other, dependent on society. We all seek societal acceptance or differently put, we want to love and be loved and in order to get to this point many of us have aligned our standard to fit into societal and cultural beliefs.

We love to blend in, to feel among. We do not want to be the odd one out so much so that many of us have lost our identity in the pursuit of happiness that comes from societal acceptance. We have lost our brands, those things that make us unique and significant. We lost them all in a bid to get the nod and approval of people around us. Many of us have found ourselves in the place of trying to understand ourselves and understanding what we stand for and how it correlates with where we are.

It is in this place of self-awareness that some of us get to realise that the needs of where we are do not correlate with the needs of who we are.

The error comes from the place and time of our identity crisis or loss. Because we have followed the path laid for another and as such the needs that arise from the place where we are now and or the provision it brings does not correlate and or satisfy the needs that arise from being who we truly are. These contradictions create a situation rather unpleasant because it brings us to the place of DISEASE.

DISEASE is coined from two words

DIS – a prefix which literarily means "opposite" or "absence of".

EASE – comfort, painless, lack of difficulty.

When these two are then brought together, it tells you that disease is not just an illness, not just an organic lesion but also functional. Anything that does not function with ease within the parameters of its purpose is diseased.

You don't have to be maimed to be diseased; sometimes it just takes functioning out of position. Each time you function out of position, you can't achieve maximum and as long as you do not achieve maximum, you are diseased.

But Not Orphaned

The truth becomes that in the place of imitating others – following people without a purpose – we get out of place and function below par.

 Imagine that in a choir, a chorister who is specialised in singing tenor suddenly starts singing bass because the bass singer sounds good. Can you imagine the dysfunction that would cause?

When people dictate our pace, when we imitate people, the best we can be is second best. There is a lane on which God has put you; it is your niche where you are the best and you only compete with yourself.

A certain research was conducted with two sport teams, a senior and a junior. The coach placed all the players of the senior team out of position but organised the junior team by their strength per position. It was noted that the players of the senior team were actually the best players of the team. At the end of the day, the junior team thrashed the senior team. The question is, "why?"

But Not Orphaned

It simply could not have been due to potential ability or due to experience. It painstakingly boils down to position. Each time we operate out of position, we can never operate to full potential. I want you to know that there is a difference between surviving (adapting) and thriving. God doesn't just want you to survive; He wants you to thrive and in order to do that, you must function in your space.

Functioning in your space may sometimes mean functioning in isolation. That other people are not where you are does not make that place any less your space. That people do not support what you do does not mean that it is not what you should be doing. That people do not reason the way you do does not mean you shouldn't be reasoning so. The only prerequisite to do what you do is the conviction that you are led by the Holy Spirit. As long as you are led, rest assured that you are secured.

Let me tell you, "Everybody around you is a benefit, only God is your necessity." As long as you have God in your space, the right people will come along.

The bible puts it this way, "Seek ye first the kingdom of God and His righteousness, and all other things (including the right people) shall be added unto you."

By no means am I saying that people shouldn't be in your space. I am saying, and even philosophers and great thinkers agree, that you will always attract into your life, people and things that are in line with your dominant thought (law of attraction).

If your dominant thought be your purpose in God, people will come, who will be around you to help you in achieving that purpose.

When you are wrongly placed, the people around you will be wrongly oriented to your purpose. They will act as who they are and this will never synchronize with what you understand yourself and your journey to be. And you must understand that when you have people around who do not support your vision, it is not necessarily because they are wicked or nonchalant but maybe because you are in a misplaced environment.

Many things that appear as betrayals many times are just complications of our wrong placement.

I've seen quite a lot of people miss their destiny just because they wanted to feel among and in so doing, followed the crowd and missed the cause and course of their own lives.

God wants you to discover yourself in Him and stand with what you've discovered holding on to it and never giving up on it.

In these last days, God wants a set of people who will move in line with His design for them, who will be interested in pleasing God and not people.

Here is another reason you cannot afford to be a people follower. We all have our different identities, idiosyncratic to each individual. We all have the things we can tolerate and those we can't. If you keep trying to please everyone, your

But Not Orphaned

life will be set on Brownian motion because you'll never be able to discover yourself as your time will be spent on discovering others and how to please them. One day, after you must have wasted your very precious time, you will realise that you never actually fulfilled purpose yourself, and it would no longer matter how many people you helped fulfil their dreams.

A saying goes this way, "If you don't have a plan, you'll become a part of another's plan." And truth be told, that you are successful with another man's plan does not make you a success; it only makes that man a success.

Now, this is not to say that you cannot help people achieve their dreams or even serve other people. It is just to remind you that you must do that with the full understanding of whom you are and where you are going.

One day, I called one of my spiritual sons; he had been with me in ministry for a very long time. I do not doubt his loyalty but I had a problem with him.

But Not Orphaned

That problem was symptomatic with the fact that an assignment that usually would have taken him a day to complete now took him a week. Having observed the trend, I discovered the etiology of the syndrome, and as a medical student, I understood that it is better to treat the etiology than to just treat the symptoms.

So, I called him to a private meeting to address the etiology. The problem was in the fact that he had lost sight of the original purpose for which he was with me and once that happened, the passion could no longer be felt. This is primarily because passion is fed by purpose. Also, because he lost contact with that original purpose, he was just being my follower without a purpose hence he couldn't transition into a leader. (I do not mean position-wise because a lot of leaders put people into position who are not leaders). I mean a leader in his own right, of his own vision. I do not believe in working with anything or anybody that does not go in line with my vision.

But Not Orphaned

So I can work under anybody, but I always keep in mind the purpose of my service. Hence, even in the place of service, I make sure I lead my life, and by that I mean that I remain the driver of my actions, I understand why I do what I do. So, when I serve under you and you give instructions, I not only obey because I'm loyal but also because in doing what you asked of me, I gain experience which will be necessary to fulfilling my purpose. Thus even when I'm following you, I do that with purpose. I won't just do what you do, go where you go or say what you say as much as seeing you do them aids me with more experience because I always remember I'm me.

So, when he connected back to that original purpose, it would fuel him within the space of being himself. Hence, even when he worked with me, he wouldn't see it as working for me, but working towards accomplishing his own life goals and with that view, he'd get back his passion and hardly procrastinate on any given assignment.

But Not Orphaned

As I'm writing this book, I happen to be editing another book written by a Pastor and a friend, Pastor Louis Asandoh, titled "The Self-discovery manual." How I see it is that editing this books helps me accomplish my own plan of impacting the human race by writing and or editing any material that will make them live heaven on earth.

I am telling you this so that you will understand that it doesn't matter how much of my co-workers in ministry I serve or how many people I help edit their books, if I do not have a purpose of doing that, I am still a failure because I am not fulfilling a purpose within me.

This is one reason why a lot of active people still do not find a sense of fulfilment irrespective of how much time and energy they have invested in a lot of projects.

John, a young boy, was given chores to do at home by his parents while they were leaving for work. Next-door was a lovely family with whose children John was friends so as usual, John went over to play with them and while there, the children began to do their chores. They did the dishes, dusted the furniture and beautified the living room. Of course John helped out; in fact, the beautifying of the living room was his idea and he actively participated. It was 3:30PM when they finished and John's parents were to return home by 4:00PM. Realizing that he had not done his own chores, he bolted out of his friends' house and headed home. As you may have guessed, his parents returned to meet the house in a mess. If you were John's parents, what would you do?

You'd agree with me that it doesn't matter how much energy John had expended, the creative ideas he doled out or how good a job he'd done next-door, he was still a failure at what'd ha had been appointed to do.

I don't know how much you've achieved in a misplaced environment that makes you work hard but reap bad, I don't care how long you've spent cultivating other people's fields while yours remain untilled, I want you to know that it is not too late

But Not Orphaned

to get things right. Jesus said he won't leave you comfortless and so he is calling you again to come back to your own place of responsibility where He'll comfort you and give you the strength and speed to recover from the years the locusts of misplacement have eaten.

CHAPTER 3

YOUR LIFE, YOUR PRIORITY

Earlier on in this book, I asked: "Who is responsible for the outcome of a man? His situations, the people around him or himself? I think we're now at the point where we need to answer that question with all honesty.

The truth, my dear, is that YOU ARE RESPONSIBLE FOR YOUR LIFE.

In life, what happens to you, what people do to you, is important but I tell you that much more important is how you choose to react or respond to those things. Our lives are decided mainly by our response to situations and people.

I often tell people that "life is a drama where people act and react."

Usually, it is reactions that set the tone for the final situation which then many times gives the definition to the overall situation.

But Not Orphaned

August 24, 2014 was Independence Day celebration in Ukraine and I had just transferred from Crimea to Lviv the month before. On the said day, I went with a mentee to McDonalds at around 9:30PM to get some items and on returning home, as we made to open the main gate leading into my apartment, we were accosted by three Ukrainian boys, the oldest of whom looked about twenty years old; they attempted to mug us and we pleaded that they let us be all to no avail. My mentee – infuriated by the situation and feeling that by size and age, they were no match for us – tried to force his way through and earned himself a punch in the face. As he made to retaliate, I stopped him and insisted that we walk away as fast as we could.

There were three things I thought about before making that decision:

1. If we engaged in a fight with them, there was no saying what weapons they carried and the extents to which they could go, such as killing us and running away. Being black

and a foreigner in Ukraine, not only would one die prematurely but also without justice.

2. In the event that we beat them, they could trail us to our residence and in the future, lay an ambush for us with the rest of their gang.

3. Had we overpowered them, the Ukrainian legal system is so rotten that we would have been victimized and branded the bad guys. Had we claimed self-defence, the police wouldn't even hear any of it.

To further confirm this, we immediately went to a nearby hotel and called the police severally and to our chagrin, there was no reply.

Now, that day could have ended differently had we not responded differently. There is a vicious cycle that deals with situation and response mechanism.

But Not Orphaned

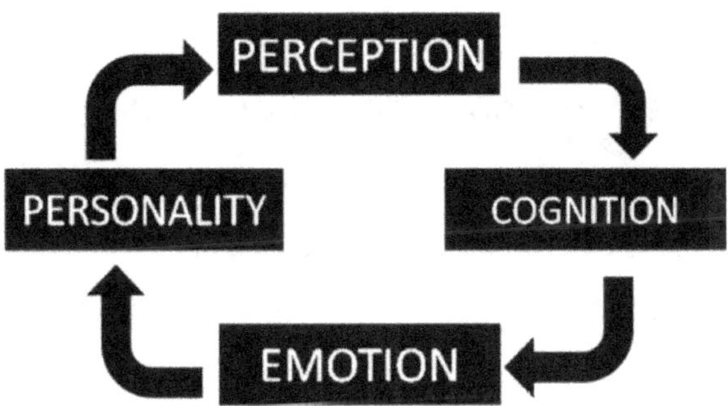

Perception is basically the way we regard, understand and interpret things and situations. Perception, I believe, is dependent on your personality. It is commonly said and I agree, that many times we do not see things and people the way they are but rather the way we are. If you are used to slapping your friends on the head, the day one of them tries to stretch his hand for something that is directly behind your head, you will almost impulsively try to duck before you realise he does not intend to hit you.

The reason you duck is not because of the situation but your flawed perception as a result of your personality.

But Not Orphaned

I believe there are two levels of perception, which are based on subjection to cognition. Hence, if I subject a matter to cognition, it can provide me with a different emotion which will give me an instant personality that in turn will give me a new perspective.

I'll give you an analogy shortly but first, let's talk cognition.

Cognition is a complex of mental activity that involves attention, memory, evaluation and judgement. However, as complex as it sounds, cognition can take place within seconds.

It is worthy of note that cognition is knowledge based because the knowledge you have becomes the standard against which what you are trying to analyse is measured.

I had earlier told you of the story of my mentee and me. What I did was to subject the situation to cognition. I thought about the "what ifs" and "what if-nots" and I was able to come to a reasonable conclusion only because I knew the state of the Ukrainian legal system and the possibility of those boys being armed with dangerous weapon. Had I not known better, the result of my cognition would most definitely have been different.

The basis of this book is to remind you that you are not alone in any given situation; to remind you that God is with you and all you need to do is to be with God, because two cannot work together unless they agree. But perhaps if you didn't know this, there would be nothing for you against which you could analyse situations to conclude that God is yet good. If you do not have a knowledge that everything works together for good to them that love God and are called according to His purpose, you'll not have a base against which you can pitch your situation to see if they match or add up.

Cognition may be rightly seen as the basis for our emotions, personality and perception.

Proverbs 23:7a

For as he thinketh in his heart, so is he.

But Not Orphaned

Practically, after I had lost my parents, the natural perception was to be dejected but then I subjected that perception to cognition. Note that I had prior become embodied with the right knowledge. In my cognition, memory brought to me that all things work together for my good. Memory brought to me that even if mothers abandon their suckling babes, He – the Lord – would never forsake me. Memory brought to me that I have never seen the righteous forsaken or His children beg for bread. So my situation could not withstand the strength of the knowledge of God I had inside me. Hence the outcome of that cognition changed my emotions.

Emotion is an intuitive feeling that can be derived from circumstances (shallow) and/or knowledge-based reasoning/cognition (deep).

Because my emotion had been directed towards a constant path, it necessitated that I maintained an awesome personality.
My personality – if at all it changed – only got better because I had a new perception, one

different from the natural and immediate perception that my situation would have otherwise entailed.

If you reconsider the circle, you'll find out basically that your cognitive process is directly responsible for the outcome of your personality.

The bible has this to say in

Philippians 4:8

Finally, brethren, whatsoever things are true, whatsoever things are honest, whatsoever things are just, whatsoever things are pure, whatsoever things are lovely, whatsoever things are of good report; if there be any virtue, and if there be any praise, think on these things.

It is because what you place your mind on shapes the direction of your cognition.

God wants to you to keep feeding your spirit with His word so that your spirit in turn can feed your soul, the development of your soul, a component of which is your mind is directly proportional to your growth in life. Until you grow, you will never learn to take responsibilities, you'll always blame anything and everything for your circumstances.

You must learn to develop and build yourself, I have always said the height of a man's thought is the limit of his being and to know that you are as limited in thought as the limit of the parameters of your thinking which is what you know, you cannot reason outside of what you know.

As the leader of one of the movements I was involved in, so many times I had to allow some people who were subject to me have the upper hand, on so many occasions I had to let go of my ego for the greater good, one of the local association presidents then would go on to challenge me unnecessarily in what at that time appeared to be a power tussle. May be someday I would be able to go into full details of how I was vehemently opposed by the very person I thought would support me most. But one thing stood out I knew there is a problem if my ego was bigger than my dream. So it was a very easy decision for me. I

But Not Orphaned

also knew power and even life itself is transient as I always tell people "one day we all will be former; former this, former that" at the end of the day what will be remembered of us will be what we achieved while we held sway. While it must be stated that I have never in my life been a man of perfect character, I do err too but one must also appreciate the fact that I am always working on myself by the use of the word. Every night (except for a few cases when I sleep off unexpectedly) before I go to bed I engage my conscience as I go through my day and how it went, searching all my action and inactions, I most times know what/how I was wrong and by God's grace get better with those things. I say this because I have learnt that wealth and power corrupts but I have also learnt that it corrupt people whose character was never indeed built before possessing either money or power, this was proven to me when I saw the very one I could testify to the warmth of his character become so vociferous that it was as though I didn't know him before. As much as I do not want to sacrifice him on the altar of my opinion I still feel if

But Not Orphaned

he had taken time to build himself, power wouldn't matter. In one of his typical rage he said to me in a conversation he never knew was recorded for futuristic purpose he said to me I'm spiritual but not Godly" while threatening to deal with me. As I sat and watched him I couldn't but wonder if anger was responsible for making such a statement and many more but then I realized again that anger is only an emotions that emboldens one to pour out even the deepest part of the heart.

What I am trying to tell you with this is that you cannot afford to stop working on your mind, developing your character. Capacity can get you anywhere in life but only character can keep you. Character is built by a continuous development of cognition which will help you build a better perspective and that perspective with the emotion that comes along with it is what determines your personality which in this case one can equate to your character.

But Not Orphaned

Between 2011-2014, God has brought some very annoying people my way, one was so annoying that I contemplated letting go of our friendship on the basis of my ego being always hurt, but somehow I decided I was going to stay and learn self-control from it. And believe me it did work. I have not learnt how not to get angry anymore but I have learnt how not to stay angry and how not to let anyone drill into me using anger as a tool. Today I can manage anger not because I took a course on it but because I changed my perspective.

our cognition is no doubt shaped by our perspective, If you begin to face every little challenge you have now with grace and understanding that they can build character in you, not only will you overcome, you'd also grow.

Your cognition is so important, it determines if you will play victim to any given circumstance or face it like a victor. Your cognition decides if you will stay strong or you will crumble.

But Not Orphaned

Feed yourself with the right material, surround yourself with the right people, do your best to engage in analytic discussions and very soon you'd see yourself becoming the better version of you.

The two perspective then becomes

1. Pre-cognition
2. Post-cognition

Pre-cognition Perspective: is your default perspective, it is impulsive, it is your raw unprocessed receptor, it determines the primary way your react or respond to things. It is also important to know that after every process of cognition that helps you build a new perspective, there is every possibility that this de novo perspective becomes your pre-cognition perspective in the next situation

Post-cognition Perspective: this is the most important, because it is most likely going to determine your next line of action, you can judge the level of your person by your post-cognition perspective because it is decided by the height of your cognition, this means that you can't have a better perspective than how you think.

The power of perspective is so much that it basically determines if two can work together, have you ever been in a situation where you have reasoned out a particular plan and after presenting it, the people to whom you present it just cannot see things in your perspective? How did you feel?

It is true that you may have to see it in their own perspective but what happens if you just can't not because you're proud but because it's a lower perspective?

As much as you'd have to compromise to let them have it their way especially if you're within a corporate organization where you're not the head but if it keeps happening that way you will agree with me that deep down within you'd begin to discover that is not the best environment to work.

Working with people who have a fixed perspective, people who do things a certain way because that is how it has always been done, can simply be frustrating.

Certainly one can equate perspective to mental freedom or mental slavery, in the book "the winning edge" by Oluwole Femi I contributed a piece titled mental slavery which I'd like to share with you.

MENTAL SLAVERY

One thing that has ever caught my attention so wildly is an experiment conducted on a bee, the bee was placed in a jar and the jar was closed with a lid, the bee tries to fly out, but each time it does, it hits it's the lid, this process had colonized the mind of the bee not to go beyond a level for the fear of hitting its head against the jar after few minutes the lid was taken off, now the jar was open, but the bee never went beyond that level, so it remained in the jar not because the lid was there but because it was not aware the lid was off, most times we as people are held to ransom not by anything more than the ignorance of our own

But Not Orphaned

minds, Man live by his outlook, but a right outlook, is only brought about by a right in-look, just like the bee many people live in mental slavery; mental slavery is the inability to view things or even one's self differently from previous commonly accepted fate, happenings or belief.

To be enslaved is to be deprived of one's freedom and expressions, so when it is now mental, it depicts though the presence but independence this type of slavery from an external force, though may be induced by the external but is only permitted by the internal, I've had the opportunity to man a blog and also a facebook page, their privacy settings were made strict such that all your post must pass through an administrator before they appear on the page, this is exactly what mental slavery is, though the influence may be from the outside but the result depends on the within. Just like I as an administrator is responsible for every post that appears on the page so is every man responsible for what goes on in his mind, one of the greatest ability of a man is that he can

But Not Orphaned

decide what he wants to think, that is why the greatest victory against a man is the capture of the mind, in this world of immerse competition it is a known fact that if you do not control your mind someone else will do that for you, Even after independence, there is no truly independent African nation today, not because there is a gun to their head, European nations have resources, but Africa has blood resources and the problem is that the people have been subjected to mental slavery. The scripture says "as a man thinketh in his heart so is he" the freedom of your being is dependent on the freedom of your mind As I was walking one blissful noon, "God said to me the height of your thinking is the limit of your being" that triggered me to start seeing things differently, just as slavery is in levels, the fact that all seems to be well just does not mean you are not a victim of mental slavery, that you are the chief slave does not mean you are a freeman. The mind is subject to the law of use and disuse, the more you use it the powerful it becomes, the only thing stronger than a powerful mind is a courageous heart, but a

But Not Orphaned

courageous heart is an offspring of a mental liberty I've also heard that in caging an elephant you tie it's leg to a tree making the rope as long as the perimeter around which you want it to move, then after sometimes, months maybe you remove it, it is said that the elephant will never move out because it is not aware the rope has been taking off, you'll never go beyond your limit if you quit trying to. It is mental slavery to think the highest you could ever do has been done by someone else, One of the institution regrettably that breeds and builds minded invalids today is the school, all the school teaches is mediocrity, the school teach a total percentage of 100 students that pass through it how to survive through life, and pitiably only a handful of these students understand how to soar in life parting the others to become educated illiterates, Thomas Jefferson said "I prefer a dangerous freedom to a peaceful slavery" I have come to discover that there are a lot of things that are acceptable to my mates but are not to me, so as you try to fight out your liberty from mental slavery never expect your neighbour to see you as sane, because what you are doing, is not just what he has not seen before but probably what he has never thought Remember, mental freedom is the father to mental expression which begot physical freedom a father to physical expression that drives the wheels of success.

CHAPTER 4

HE DIDN'T LEAVE ME ORPHANED

While I would easily agree that growing up wasn't all rosy for me, as I had the mixed experience of abundance and lack; some days we had all we wished for and other days, not so much, through it all, I learnt family values and what they really meant.

Like I often say in humour, "my family was more nuclear than a nuclear reactor". By that, I mean that my siblings and I were not exposed to an extended family, which is the normal African definition of family. I suppose this was due to my parents' experiences growing up but their decision invariably meant that most of the love I received growing up was from my parents, that should be the case but as a grown man now exposed to different societies and cultures I have come to learn that the love of relatives is a bad idea, anyway little can be done to undo that now and one has to believe that my parents did what they believed was right within the context of what was their reality then.

I was raised with certain values that have helped stabilize me and aided my development as a man and responsibility was one of those.

As early as the age of twelve, during the holidays, my father made me responsible for the sale of soft drinks which included fruit juices, carbonated drinks and a variety of other refreshing non-alcoholic drinks in his pharmacy shop. I would buy these at discounted wholesale prices and sell at retail prices such that at the end of the day, whatever gain I made was mine to keep. Roy, my eight year old brother who was responsible for the sale of water – bottled water, sachet water (pure water in Nigerian terms) – operated the same way that I did.

Our parents not only taught us to be resourceful by this means, but they also taught us to make thrift donations, which helped us to save money so that the possession of money didn't make us consumer minded. I was able to make a daily thrift of between 1000 to 1500 Naira, depending on how much sale I made for that day. This meant that at the end of the holiday, I was able to save about 30000 to 40000 Naira. My parents helped us to deposit in our trust-fund. For this reason, I hardly remember asking my father for "pocket" money.

This also helped me understand what it means to make money at an early age. It opened my mind for entrepreneurship and skill acquisition and this is what became the substratum of my philosophy

"PREPAREDNESS IS THE MAJOR DOOR OPPORTUNITY KNOCKS ON."

Using this as a guide I have gone ahead to learn skills ranging from photography to Pastry making (I think you should eat one of my cakes) and these skill have at sundry times provided me money when I was in dire need. Once I saw a need in the hostel where I used to live, Students had too many dirty rugs and the only solution was to buy a new one, the entrepreneur in me helped them solve that problem by becoming a "Rug Cleaner" and all I needed to do was to look for a car-wash negotiated with the proprietor, he comes for the rugs and returns them while I get the money, pay him his part and held on to mine. I had just become the saviour of many students whilst making money for myself at almost no cost on me save the packing of the rug.

It is my belief that the reason opportunity doesn't come is either of these:

1. I haven't built a door for it to knock on.
2. I am not in the place where it knocks.
3. It is knocking but I haven't heard.

From this, I also learnt to be independent and not see myself as one to whom anyone was indebted. I don't feel entitled. And in the case that someone gives me anything, I see it as a privilege and not a right. This has helped me build gratitude as an attitude.

This empowerment by my parents meant that my days of abundance outnumbered my days of lack.

But Not Orphaned

As a matter of fact, every gadget I have ever used apart from the laptop that my mother gave me for my 17th birthday was purchased with my money. I knew the value of money and I developed the attitude of never asking for money unless it was very necessary. Truthfully, it's a rare act among my peers, most of who feel it is their fundamental right (which isn't entirely false). It is a philosophy inherited by my generation, called generational duty.

A situation where generation C expects generation B to take care of them because generation A took care of generation B. Hence, they make demands, only to grow up and realize that it isn't as easy as it seemed.

Most people grow to appreciate the efforts of their ever-hardworking parents only when they themselves have gotten into the labour market and tried to make ends meet.

As I grew older, I began to appreciate even more the seeds that my parents had sown in me both

But Not Orphaned

spiritually and morally. While they became emotionally absent through their death and that part no one could fill, they had instilled in me virtues that reminded me that they were just – in my mother's words – "caretakers."

I grew to understand that my parents were just a channel and not the source and that my resources could only come from my source, irrespective of what/who the channel is.

My intention for writing this is to let you know that even after I had lost the only channel that I knew, resources did not stop locating me.

About a week after my mother passed away, I was to receive a little sum of money for upkeep which had been delayed due to her inability to send, but I had lost my ATM card and so I opted to use the account of my good friend, Ojo Anuoluwapo, in which he already had a sum of money. When my money came in, I took the card from him and went straight to the nearest ATM machine that was dispensing (It was a time when trade restriction had started to bite in Crimea) and instantly, I had the urge to punch in an amount I knew was not in the account. Actually, the figure was about one and a half times more than my money and his put together. So, as I punched in the digits and pressed continue, I was shocked to my bones to see the machine dispensing. With the crowd behind me, as that was the only ATM dispensing in that area, I was overwhelmed but I had to check the balance because I had just withdrawn an amount so big that if I gave my friend his money which he hadn't even instructed me to withdraw, I'd still have enough.

So I checked the account to see that there was still money left, more than my friend's initial balance. Of course, the next thing was to ask my brother if he had sent me more than he initially declared to me but he answered in the negative.

This miracle came at the time I needed it most. In about two weeks, my ministry was to hold her third conference and there were many bills to settle. This money helped me settle all and I was still left with enough to buy some personal effects.

This is what I call my ATM miracle. After the conference was over, the next challenge was to transfer out of the Crimea peninsula to Ukraine mainland. It was a challenge because I wasn't financially capable. Tuition in Crimea State Medical University was dollars 3500 but in Lviv National Medical University to which I was transferring, it was 4300 dollars. One must first be sure of where 3500 dollars will come from before thinking of how to get the extra 800 dollars.

More challenging was the fact that I still owed a part of my hostel fee, which I had to pay before I could sign out of the university.

I could not even boast of $50. I tried to sell a few valuables that I couldn't take to my intended new environment, so as to raise a little money but even that didn't work as so many other students were equally transferring and were selling their property as well. The situation was not conducive or

But Not Orphaned

convenient to the ordinary man. However, I tell you, there was this inexplicable peace on my inside, an assurance that swept away worries. Let me tell you, "When you know God is with you, you'll sweat over nothing."

A cascade of favour began to overwhelm me, beginning from a parent's visit for her daughter's graduation that summer. Tope – the said daughter – and I had become friends towards the end of her study and thanks to my relationship with her roommate who was the vice-president of the Nigerian students' association where I was the public relations officer, we had become quite close. More so, around this time, I was a regular in their room, learning the skills of bakery, as the duo were prolific in the art, having run their co-owned E&T bakery for some years.

It turned out that Tope had told her mother about me, who upon her departure gave me through her daughter, a sum of money that was enough to settle my debt in the school and transport me out of Crimea.

But Not Orphaned

In my utmost gratefulness to her, this was another reminder that as long as God remained my source, He would always deliver resources to me via any channel of His choice.

Coming to Lviv, I was required to make a down payment of 10% of the tuition fee before I would be accepted; that was $430, excluding the accommodation. I didn't have the money, but because of the political situation and the urge in my spirit to leave Crimea, I was willing to risk "hanging" in mainland Ukraine through the holiday till I got registered by September if I couldn't do it earlier.

Since Mrs Opanuga (Tope's mother) had helped me overcome the first step, I signed out and got into the train headed for Lviv. However, while in the train, I decided against going directly to Lviv, as I had no assurance of accommodation. Hence, I alighted in Vinnitsa, having called my friend, Pastor Louis Ngwa. I spent with him a week, one which saw the continuation of my favour cascade as God began to use people all round to meet my needs and by the end of that week, I had enough money to offset 30% of my tuition fee and to tend to my welfare through the summer holidays. God had also strategically placed some people, who stood, and still stand rock-solid behind me.

Lade Adepoju was one of such people, who just knew when to reach me. It was as though she was a regulator of my feedback mechanism. Many times when I expected nothing from her, she proved to be the answer to my prayers.

There are too many financial answers that God has brought my way and there has always been a resounding lesson:

"Be nice and respectful to the people you come across. You never know who you helper could be."

A certain Yoruba adage says, "Ajumobi o kan ti anu, eni Oluwa ran sini lo nseni loore." This means, "family ties is no guarantee for favour, it is he who God sends your way that favours you." This has particularly been the case for me.

But Not Orphaned

Even in Lviv where I had just relocated to, at times I would get envelopes addressed to me by unknown persons. Some would walk up to me and deliver their parcels often with lines like, "God placed it in my heart to give this to you." With help from above delivered through channels on earth, both familiar and not, I was able to complete the tuition for my 4th year of medical school. So I encourage you to learn a skill, it may one day prove to be the saving grace

 I must say that skill acquisition helped me cushion the effect of many broke days as many times the only saving grace was the fact that I baked cakes to sell, and also I do photography.

The next challenge was one that promised to be interesting. I had officially become the president of the Nigerian Students' Association Ukraine, while I was still in the ministry. The thought of the financial responsibility that was upon me just would not go away but I had learnt how to "spirit storm."

But Not Orphaned

Spirit storming is my way of critical thinking while speaking in tongues. I allow my spirit to communicate with God while I get my paper and pen ready believing that I will get an answer to the particular issue for which I am spirit storming.

Spirit storming is what I resort to when all critical thinking and analysis have failed me.

I am one who believes that God gave us brains so that we do not disturb Him all the time. However, I also believe in being directed by God and that there are certain situations, around which our minds cannot wrap. These situations ordinarily would cause apprehension, but having related with God for as long as I had, spirit storming was and still is my way out.

This particular week, I had felt a strong push in my spirit to change my environment for the weekend. This I did and while on the bed in my friend's house, I had an Idea whilst spirit storming. I shared this idea with a few people I knew cared about me and the result of the idea was financial empowerment. I was financially empowered to pay my tuition fee and finance the association over which I presided. I could also contribute to the ministry, which in itself wasn't much of a weight on me because of our ever loyal and growing partners.

Again I say to you challenges must not stop your vision. Even if you do not receive support or succour from anyone, just keep your faith in God and I can tell you with authority and confidence that everything will work together for your good.

In all of these again I learnt the power of mastering principles, I understood that it takes miracle to keep whatever miracle gives and so I have gone and I'm going all out to learn the secrets of the rich, to gain financial literacy, to have a financial plan because while God was providing via several miracles I discovered that living in abundance was better. And maybe I really can't do much about it now but I sure know I can secure the future by learning the important principles needed for financial freedom today so that my next testimony would be I moved from MIRACLES TO BLESSINGS. I believe if you too today while still waiting on God for your miracle begin to expand your knowledge and acquire information that will develop your mind you may just discover your miracle and indeed the understanding to preserve it and turn it into a blessing.

In my meditation and thinking over how God has been good to me and how far He has brought me, a thought came to mind. Was this all predestination?

The simple answer is that while predestination could be a huge contributing factor, my decision to be resilient, to believe and to obey what God's word says about me is to be very much considered. It is worthy of note that if I had given up in my times of trouble when the storm was strongest, I wouldn't have become what I could have become (which I eventually became and I still am in the process of becoming). Also noteworthy is the principle of resilience, a resilience that defies the possible outcome of events but stays deeply rooted in its insurance – in my case, God. I deal with this extensively in my book titled *REDIFINING FAITH*.

There is a lot to tell about me as there is a lot I've been through but the excellency of it all is that today as you are reading through the pages of this book, I can boldly declare to you that it doesn't matter the strength of the storm that comes to rock your boat neither does it matter the size of your boat in comparison to the storm as long as you've got Jesus in the boat with you.

Storms are mighty but Jesus is the almighty. I do not doubt the potency of your challenge but I want to remind you through my story that Jesus is omnipotent.
He may not solve your problem with the method you are familiar with, He may operate outside the scope and parameters of your knowledge and beyond what your mind can fathom but know that just because you do not understand doesn't mean He isn't at work.

But Not Orphaned

Maybe you do find this contradictory to what the bible says in

Proverbs 23:18

For surely there is an end; and thine expectation shall not be cut off.

But I guarantee you that the power of this verse lies in what your expectation is. The word "expectation" (tik-vaw in Hebrew) means "cord" literally and "hope" figuratively. Literally translated, that verse would read, "Your anchor (cord) shall not be cut off."
The question is: on what/who is your chord anchored? On things or God?

If it be on things, then you surely must hold things responsible for the fulfilling of this verse but I want to believe that things do not make and cannot fulfil promises. But if your cord (hope) be anchored on God, then you hold God by who He is. Which brings us to another question, who is He to you? A healer, a provider, a comforter, a lover?

But Not Orphaned

Who He is to you will certainly depend on who you are to Him, because a relationship takes two. To me, He is a father and because He is my father, He knows what is best for me and gives it to me at the right time and this is why like David, I can boldly declare, "The lord is my shepherd, I shall not want!"

As a sheep in his pasture, He knows what grass I need to eat; I trust Him to decide what is best. My cord is tied to Him and my expectation is on His person rather than on the things He can do as a person. Hence my expectation shall not be cut off. Let me say it this way, "The lord is my Portion."

When the bible says "if you ask anything, you shall receive" one must ask anything? How shall I ask for what I can't handle and a loving God will give it to me. A treasure can become an injurious weapon in the hand of one who cannot handle it. So I have understood that the asking isn't an impulsive asking, it isn't even an emotional asking, it is a spirit led one, that is why the basis of all the asking you and I should make is upon our growing relationship with God.

Solomon offered sacrifice to God, and in night God appeared to him in a dream, my question to you is how intellectual are you when you are unconscious? I'm glad you have the answer. So the next question is how can a sleeping man make demands of and from God?

It is quite simple, all God requires from you is your sacrifice (relationship as it were) and He himself will lead you beside the still waters and that is why scripture says the spirit himself helps our infirmities by making intersessions for us with groaning that cannot be uttered. And for everyday of your relationship you move from the place of petition to the place of communing with God.

Many times we pray (petition) when we're meant to be out taking responsibilities just because we're not led, being led makes you to the door and ask for a key but many of us keep praying (petitioning) for a room and expecting a key to drop from heaven without ever being sensitive to the leading of God and following that. If we will choose today to be relationship conscious as opposed to getting "something" from God conscious, only then will we begin to see the reality in "if you ask, you shall receive".

My earnest prayer for you is that from today you will be more desirous of God, that you may gain for yourself an experiential knowledge of him for it is in that experiential knowledge that you like me will find comfort for all of your situations, answers to your problems, it is in that relationship that you get double for your trouble and grace for every place you were once scheduled to be disgraced.

But not orphaned as it pertains to me is the story of a boy who refused to be defined by his situation, who refused to be defined by his environment, it is the story of one who realised the power of the relationship with God and taking responsibility, once I heard Pastor Henry Madava say "God will only deliver to you the things/places for which you take responsibilities" so as you read

But Not Orphaned

this book one important decision you must make is
never to resign to fate, never to be defined by your
circumstance, take responsibility and stay with
God and in no time you will receive comfort for
your soul.

I commit you unto God and the word of his grace
which is able to build you up and give you an
inheritance among the saints.

BONUS ARTICLE

TRADITIONS, INDIVIDUALITY AND GENERATIONAL SHIFT

One Friday, I had a chat with my surgery lecturer about the gastrointestinal effect of an Ukrainian food called ropox (garox), history with this food for me dates down to year 2011, a meal after which I became best of friends with my toilet bowl. An experience that did not elude most of my friends I introduced to the food.

After the discussion my lecturer told me consequentially to me telling him that I had stopped consuming this product, that he also disliked some food even from childhood and hence refrained from them, one of which was Onion. As I was there sitting I got lost in my thoughts, the theme of which was TRADITIONS.

Defined by Merriam-Webster dictionary to be a way of thinking, behaving, or doing something that has been used by the people in a particular group,

family, society, etc., for a long time.
It suddenly dawned on me that being the head of his family, there was every possibility that one item called onion may be missing in the meal recipes and hence his children grow up not eating onions, and their children too. This trend can be passed down through generations without a particular generation understanding why.

I have a taste of this myself, I just won't eat pork. It was never served in household I grew up. I'm sure you also can relate to this with your experiences.

TRADITION AND INDIVIDUALITY

Albeit I do not discredit the importance of tradition to some people, I do challenge its grip on our freedom to choose. The question being should I be constrained by the choice of another man who could have chosen otherwise? In simpler terms should I because my father does not like pork not also eat if I'm ever want to? This I call the problem of individuality.

TRADITION AND GENERATIONAL SHIFT.

But Not Orphaned

As we well know that as generations come and go so does the changes it brings, hence the debate becomes that of Dogma and Paradigm. Is it not anti-normal if we do not flow with the generational shift, if we hold certain principles in dogmatism? How then do we preserve our familial idiosyncrasy if we do not?

BONUS ARTICLE

LAWS OF DECISION

One vital thing you will agree with me that is a great challenge to you and I is decision. Sometimes the problem lies in making them, other times in effecting them. Either way we get to points where we can surely say that the singular process of decision is just what stands between us and particular targets, be it who or what.

Decision is not just the result of a long or short term cognition but most importantly a reflection of one's personality.

in a way to help you make decisions, I have come up with certain laws of decision

1ST LAW OF DECISION
DECIDE TO DECIDE

your life today is a result of your yester-decisions, you may say "I really did not decide all these" yeah, I know exactly how you feel but you must understand that INDECISION IS A DECISION NOT TO DECIDE and so your decision not to decide is responsible for your state now at least. No matter what options life bring along, though they be variables but life itself is constant and time will

But Not Orphaned

always move so therefore when you decide not to decide, one of these options still becomes your reality.

Most times the ones we just really don't want, so it is better to make your decisions irrespective of how difficult it may appear.

To be experienced in something you must partake in it, so never be afraid of making the wrong choice, it only teaches you one way it won't work. You have to learn to be the driver of your own life because no one else knows your destination but you.

You must decide to decide thus making you responsible not just for but also in your life.

2ND LAW OF DECISION
NEVER GO FOR THE SHORT TERM

Sometimes after we've made what seemed to be the most brilliant decision of a life time, we just discover that the whole brilliant idea is working against the purpose for which it was set up, this is not necessarily because the decision was bad but rather because it was not reinforced with a set up for futuristic purpose, it is just like building a good road during the dry season and not constructing a drainage, when rain comes it doesn't matter how good the road is or was, it just will be not good for motor activities due to flood.

Every time you have to make decisions always consider the long term conquest rather than the short term victories.

Before you finalize any decision, try to ask yourself, what will be the impact of this decision in the long term?

Avoid being caught in the web of your own decisions.

But Not Orphaned

3RD LAW OF DECISION

PLAY THE PLAYER NOT THE CARDS

Ceteris paribus (all things being equal), all the choices you have in life even at a time may not be favourable, all odds may be against you, but here is one thing I've learnt from a poker game, a very strict rule "you do not play the cards you play the player.

Of course this does not mean you are not playing the cards. Playing the player is just more important.
How does this apply? You must understand that the game and the player is constant while the card is variable in which case the cards represent your options in decision making and the player, in each case life.

No matter what your options and choices are, life goes on. So you have to be smart enough to decipher the life around you, what is and what may be about it.

But Not Orphaned

The life around you is peculiar to you alone, though the options are the same, do not be surprised if we both pick the same option (card) but yet we have different result, the reason is clear, the players (life around) are different. Learn to master the life around you, the options will then be just a compliment no matter what they are. In every decision you have to make, always remember that all you are trying to do is to beat what life threw at you. Life is your competitor so learn to play the player and not the card.

Bamisaye Victor

BUT NOT ORPHANED

From Despair to Inspire

Signed for publication 07/18/2016
Format 64x90/16. Offset Paper. Offset.
The headset is Times New Roman.
Conventional printing pages 6,75.
Accounting and publishing pages 6.28.
Circulation 1000 copies. Order number 15365.

Printed from the original customer.
FOP Korzun D.Yu.
21027, a / c 8825, c. Vinnytsia, st. 600-year anniversary, 21.
Tel .: (0432) 603-000, 69-67-69.

Publisher and manufacturer LLC "Nilan-LTD"
Certificate of entry the subject of publishing in the State
Register of publishers, manufacturers and distributors of publishers,
manufacturers and distributors series ДК № 4299 from 04.11.2012
21027. PO Box 8825, c. Vinnytsia, st. 600-year anniversary, 21.
Tel .: (0432) 603-000, 69-67-69.
e-mail: info@tvoru.com.ua
http://www.tvoru.com.ua